I Can Read About®
Sharks

I Can Read About
Sharks

Written by C.J. Naden
Illustrated by Paul Lopez

SCHOLASTIC INC.

New York Toronto London Auckland Sydney
Mexico City New Delhi Hong Kong Buenos Aires

ISBN 0-439-63625-6

Text copyright © 1996 by Troll Communications L. L. C.
Illustrations copyright © 1996 by Paul Lopez. All rights reserved.
Published by Scholastic Inc. SCHOLASTIC and associated logos are trademarks
and/or registered trademarks of Scholastic Inc.

12 11 10 9 8 7 6 5   4 5 6 7 8 9/0

Printed in the U.S.A.   08

First Scholastic printing, January 2004

SHARK!
The word makes people shudder. A shark will attack anything—
small fish, big fish, people, and even boats.

Is the shark really so dangerous?
What do we know about this creature?

We know the shark is a meat-eating fish. It eats live or dead sea animals, and almost anything else. Some strange things have been found in the stomachs of sharks—everything from old junk to giant turtles.

The shark is one of the world's best swimmers.
Its sleek body moves swiftly through the sea. Some
sharks can swim over 40 miles (64 kilometers) an hour.

dorsal

pectoral

dorsal

caudal fin

Their strong
tails give them
power. Their side, or
pectoral, fins give them balance.
Most sharks have two back, or dorsal, fins. The
larger one is nearer the head. It is shaped like a triangle.
When this pointed fin cuts through the water, danger is near.

A shark does not see as well as it hears or smells.
But in clear water, it can see something moving from
50 feet (15 meters) away. Like other fish, the shark can feel
something moving without seeing it.

Sharks are not considered very smart. But they have a keen sense of smell, and they hear well. These senses—plus their swimming speed—make them very good hunters and dangerous killers.

JAWS!
The shark has huge jaws and sharp teeth. The jaws of the white shark are so strong that they can bite a person in half. Shark teeth grow in several rows. And the shark doesn't have to worry about losing a tooth. Another just moves up to replace it!

The shark is a fish, but it is different
from most fish in many ways. The shark has rough skin.
Its skin is tough and is covered with scales that look like
very tiny teeth. Sharkskin feels like sandpaper.

The eggs of most sharks hatch inside the mother's body. Baby sharks are called *pups*. They are born alive.

The pups must take care of themselves right away. The parents don't take care of them at all. Sometimes the parents even eat them!

A shark does not have any bones. Its skeleton is made of cartilage, which is tough and elastic. Most fish have a swim bladder that keeps them from sinking. But a shark does not have a swim bladder. So most sharks have to keep swimming all the time. If they don't move, they begin to sink.

Like other fish, a shark breathes through its gills. The gills of the shark are slits on each side of its head. Most fish can pump water over their gills to get oxygen. But most sharks cannot do this. Instead, a shark swims with its mouth slightly open. Water flows into its mouth and then out through its gills, taking in oxygen. So most sharks have to keep swimming in order to breathe.

We know many things about sharks. But there are many things we do not know. We do not know exactly how many kinds of sharks there are. Scientists say there are at least 350 different kinds.

long nose shark

hammerhead shark

tiger shark

whale shark

Sharks are found all over
the world, in cold water, in
warm water, in deep water, in
shallow water. Some live in fresh water.
Some sharks weigh many tons.
Some are less than a foot
(30 centimeters) in length.

There are different kinds of sharks. The *basking shark* is the second largest kind of shark. It can grow to about 30 feet (9.1 meters). It gets its name because it "basks" in the sun. It warms itself by floating near the surface of the water.

The basking shark lives in cool waters. Despite its fierce looks, it eats only tiny plants and animals called plankton. The other fish can swim by safely.

The *blue shark* gets its name from the color of its skin. It grows to about 12 feet (over 3 meters). This shark often follows ships looking for food thrown overboard. The blue shark eats fish mostly. But people should stay out of its way!

The *bull shark* often lives in fresh water. It is known to attack swimmers. The bull shark grows to about 11 feet (over 3 meters) long.

The *hammerhead shark* is found in all oceans. It is the strangest-looking member of the shark family. Its flat head looks like a hammer, with an eye and nostril at each end. It can grow to about 20 feet (6.1 meters) long. The hammerhead is very dangerous, and is often found close to shore.

SPLASH!

The *mako shark* is fast and powerful. It lives in warm tropical waters, and it grows to about 12 feet (3.7 meters). The mako may jump high out of the water if it is hooked on a fishing line. It also may attack fishing boats and swimmers.

The slow-moving *nurse shark* will attack people if they get in its way. It grows to about 14 feet (4.3 meters) long. It is yellow-brown or gray-brown in color. This shark can pump water over its gills, so it does not have to swim all the time. Sometimes the nurse shark just lies quietly on the sea bottom. It is fond of crabs and lobsters.

The *thresher shark* grows to about 20 feet (6.1 meters) long. But half of its body is its tail. This subtropical shark swims near the surface. As far as we know, it does not attack people.

The largest fish in the world is the *whale shark*.
It can grow to 49 feet (15 meters)
long. It can weigh more
than an elephant.

But this giant is harmless to people.
It eats only plankton and small fish.

WHITE SHARK!
The most dangerous and the most feared of all is the white shark. It is also called killer shark. Found in warm waters, these powerful swimmers grow to more than 21 feet (6.4 meters) long. They will attack almost anything—sea turtles, sea lions, floating logs, other sharks, and people.

It is always big news when a shark attacks a person. But sharks do not attack often. And only about 50 different types of sharks are known to attack humans at all.

Feared and
hunted, the shark has
survived in the sea for millions
of years. It is, in fact, a prehistoric
monster. Sharks of today look and act like
sharks that swam the oceans more than 100 million years ago.
Sharks have what they need to survive. They have a good body
shape for fast swimming. They have a good sense of smell for
finding food. They have strong jaws and teeth for tearing food.

Why do sharks attack moving objects? Is it because they are hungry? Are they frightened? Scientists have been studying sharks for a long time, and they are still not sure.

Scientists have tried all kinds of things to stop shark attacks. They have spread different chemicals in the water to keep sharks away. But so far, there is no one thing that works all the time with all sharks.

Scientists would also like to know why sharks have a *feeding frenzy*.
Sometimes when large groups of sharks are eating, they become very
excited. With each bite, they get more excited. Soon the sharks will
eat or bite anything in their way—boats, rubber tires, logs, anything
at all. A shark is especially dangerous during a feeding frenzy. But
scientists do not know why it starts or what it means.

To learn about sharks, scientists must get close to them.
First, they have to find the sharks. They throw chum into
the water. Chum is pieces of chopped fish, fish oil, and blood.
Scientists believe that a shark can smell blood from far away.

They wait. Then, off in the distance, a huge pointed fin cuts through the water. It is the killer of the sea, the great white shark.

Slowly, slowly it circles the boat. More chum is thrown into the water. Like a streak, the shark jumps to the surface. It snaps up 25 pounds (11 kilograms) of meat in one gulp.

Now it is
time for the
diver to go below
the surface. The diver
will study the shark
will study the shark
and take pictures. The diver is lowered in a metal cage.
But the cage will not protect the diver if the white
shark attacks. Its jaws can crunch right through the
metal. The shark can swallow the diver in one bite.

Here it comes!

The white shark has seen the diver in the cage. What will it do? Will it attack? Or will it swim silently away?

The shark slowly glides by the metal cage. Each second seems like a year to the diver. The shark keeps circling, slowly, around and around.

And then, attack! Suddenly, the shark charges the cage.
Its mouth is open, its rows of teeth bloody and bared.
The diver waits, helpless. The great mouth
comes nearer. The powerful jaws will
surely crunch the metal
bars in two.

And then,
just as suddenly,
the man-eater
turns and swims
past the cage.
In seconds, the
huge shark is gone,
disappearing into the
white churning water.

What made the shark swim away? Why did it leave the diver alone? We do not know. But the search for answers goes on. The diver is safe for another day and another dive. There will be another chance to solve the mystery of this strange creature of the sea.

Index